This book is presented to

_____

With love from

_____

Date

_____

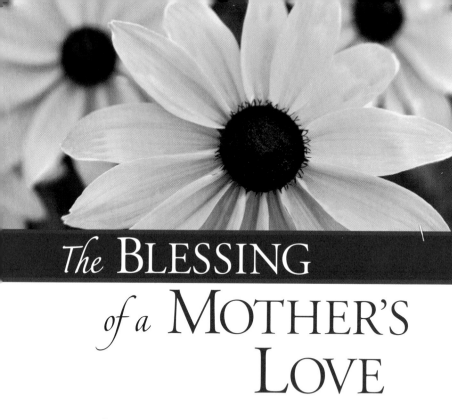

The BLESSING
of a MOTHER'S
LOVE

IDEALS PUBLICATIONS • NASHVILLE, TENNESSEE

ISBN 0-8249-5879-9

Published by Ideals Publications, a division of Guideposts
535 Metroplex Drive, Suite 250, Nashville, Tennessee 37211
www.idealsbooks.com

Printed and bound in Mexico by RR Donnelley

Compiled and edited by Peggy Schaefer
Designed by Marisa Calvin
Cover photograph by Dennis Frates

1 3 5 7 9 10 8 6 4 2

ACKNOWLEDGMENTS

CORDER, LOUISE PUGH. "A Good Mother." HOLMES, MARJORIE. "A Mother's Heart," from *McCalls* magazine, Nov. 1962.
Copyright © 1962, renewed 1990 by the author. Dystel & Goderich Literary Mgmt. KENNEDY, PAMELA. "As an only
child . . ." LIVERMORE, BETH. "Reconnecting." Copyright © 2003 by Beth Livermore from *Making Connections,* edited by
Wendy Knight. Reprinted by permission of Seal Press. LEVINE, ARLENE GAY for "It's an impossible job . . ." (originally
"A Mother's Day Grace"), used by permission of the author, and MORIKAWA, CHERYL for "Our heartbeats, notes . . ."
(originally "Mother-Daughter Song") from *Mothers and Daughters: a Poetry Celebration,* copyright © 2001 by the editor,
published by Harmony Books. ROBERTS, COKIE. "Always There" from *We Are Our Mothers' Daughters,* by Cokie Roberts.
Copyright © 1998 and 2000 by the author. Published by Perennial, an imprint of HarperCollins Publishers. Used by
permission of HarperCollins Publishers. Our sincere thanks to the following authors whom we were unable to contact: Mike
Allen and Grace Watkins. Every effort has been made to establish ownership and use of each selection in this book.
If contacted, the publisher will be pleased to rectify any inadvertent errors or omissions in subsequent editions.

Photography Credits: Page 13, Chad Ehlers/Alamy; page 15, Ace Stock Limited/Alamy; page 18–19, Trevor Smithers
ARPS/Alamy; page 21, William Johnson/Johnson's Photography; page 27, Dennis Hallinan/Alamy; page 30, Garden
Picture Library/Alamy; page 45, Andrew Wakeford/Alamy; page 46, PhotoValley/Alamy; page 49, Photo Network/Alamy;
page 54, Gay Bumgarner/Alamy; page 59, Andre Jenny/Alamy; page 61, IPS/Alamy.

WHEN GOD THOUGHT OF MOTHER,
HE MUST HAVE LAUGHED
WITH SATISFACTION
AND FRAMED IT QUICKLY—
SO RICH, SO DEEP, SO DIVINE,
SO FULL OF SOUL, POWER,
AND BEAUTY
WAS THE CONCEPTION.
—HENRY WARD BEECHER

A MOTHER'S
LOVE . . .

nurtures

She never quite leaves her children at home, even when she doesn't take them along.

—Margaret Culkin Banning

God could not be everywhere, so he created mothers.

—Jewish Proverb

IN CONSTANT DEMAND

Author Unknown

Is it not simply wonderful how many people want Mother? Is she not the most important person, the most needed person, the busiest person in all the wide world? If she is not at home, how quickly her absence is observed. If she should go to a neighbor's just for a moment, she would surely be wanted at home. If she goes out for an evening, she is probably called to the phone and told to come home quickly because the baby is sick, or Jack cut his finger, or Julia has a headache, or Pop is lonesome.

Mother has the only hands that can banish pain, the

only voice that will soothe to sleep, the only kiss that will heal the bruise, the only words that will settle disputes. She is the only one who knows where everything is kept, and so she is in constant demand, and if absent from home, is most sadly missed.

A mother is all those wonderful things you
never outgrow your need for.

—KAY ANDREW

A mother is the only person on earth who can
divide her love among ten children and each
child still have all her love.

—AUTHOR UNKNOWN

A GOOD MOTHER

Louise Pugh Corder

A good mother is the loving foundation upon which the home is built, the guardian of the small lives she has borne. Tenderly she nurtures the precious souls entrusted to her care, gratefully thanking God for the individual beauty, personality, and talents of each child and humbly praying for the wisdom and understanding to help each attain a sense of his own self-worth and special niche in God's wondrous world.

A good mother is the first and most loving teacher that her children will ever know, the most soothing nurse that

will ever attend them, their most understanding judge on earth. A good mother is her children's dearest and most faithful friend. They are always in her heart and mind, and she never ceases to sacrifice, work, and pray for what is best for them. A good mother is a shining beacon in the sea of life.

A MOTHER'S
LOVE . . .

comforts

The heart of a mother is a deep abyss, at the bottom of which you will always find forgiveness.

—Honoré de Balzac

Mother's love is peace. It need not be acquired, it need not be deserved.

—Erich Fromm

ALL THE WORLD

Washington Irving

There is an endearing tenderness in the love of a mother to a son that transcends all other affections of the heart. It is neither to be chilled by selfishness nor daunted by danger, weakened by worthlessness, nor stifled by ingratitude. She will sacrifice every comfort to his convenience; she will surrender every pleasure to his enjoyment; she will glory in his fame and exult in his prosperity; and if adversity overtake him, he will be dearer to her by misfortune; and if disgrace settle upon his name, she will still love and cherish him; and if all the world beside cast him off, she will be all the world to him.

A MOTHER'S HEART

Marjorie Holmes

A mother's heart is a many-faceted thing.

First of all, it must be like a cheery, glowing hearth to which the members of her family can always come to warm themselves, and from which they can go with their faith in themselves renewed.

But it must also be a cool and placid lake in the midst of the family storm and stress. It must be calm and undisturbed, a source of constancy, guidance, humor, and reason. . . .

It must be gentle and soft, yielding and giving, always touched by the dear, foolish gifts of feathers and dandelions and school drawings and lumpy potholders that her children bring her. It must be tender and pliant, yes . . . but, oh, it must be strong!

It must be sturdy and strong to withstand the many blows it will receive, the disappointments and things that might otherwise tear it apart; for they are the lot of every mother, no matter how hard she has tried or how fine her children may be. . . .

And so a mother's heart must be everything . . . warm and rosy, yet cool and calm . . . gentle and tender, yet dependable and strong. And though it can't be all of these things all of the time (else mothers would be saints) it manages, by some miracle, to be most of these things a great deal of the time.

For when you looked into
my mother's eyes, you knew,
as if he had told you,
why God sent her into the world—
it was to open the minds
of all who looked,
to beautiful thoughts.

—JAMES M. BARRIE

A MOTHER'S
LOVE . . .

encourages

TO FACE THE WIND

Mike Allen

I've often wondered how I came into the world so lucky. Surely, the Almighty must have looked upon the occasion with a great deal of compassion. He probably muttered something like, "That boy's mother is going to need the patience of Job and the guidance of angels." So instead of bringing Job back to life and hiring seven full-time counselors, he mustered his power and gave me Mom.

It's very hard to list even a fraction of those things that Mom means to me. She gave me roots when I thought the soil was too rocky to grow any. She opened my eyes to visions of the possible and then cheered me on as I attempted to attain them. She taught me how to laugh when I was little and how to cry when I was no longer little. When I thought I had grown too old to embrace her anymore, she patiently left her arms open so I'd have a refuge in times of need. I had thought her totally naive at times, but I have grown to find her innate wisdom a breath of fresh air in my life.

It is her heart that I love the most, for it is unlike any I have ever known. It is a heart with an unlimited capacity for love. It is a heart that affects all it touches. It is a heart that gave me wings and the confidence to fly.

I do not know how many years I will walk the lands of this planet Earth. But there is one thing I do know. I am not afraid. My mother has taught me how to face the wind.

My mother's love is larkspur,

blue and sweet,

the gentle wind

along a quiet street.

My mother's love

is little silver singing

of twilight bells,

the soft and soundless winging

of birds in flight

ACROSS AN EVENING SKY;
THE FIRST STAR, HUSHED
AND GOLD AND HIGH;
AND ON ALL PATHWAYS,
WHETHER JOY OR GRIEF,
THE CLEAR, UNWAVERING
CANDLE OF BELIEF.
—GRACE V. WATKINS

A mother is not a person to lean on but a person to make leaning unnecessary.

—Dorothy C. Fisher

Mothers give children a goal to work toward, an example to follow . . . something that gold and silver cannot buy.

—Billy Graham

THE VOICE INSIDE

Kelly Riley Baugh

My mom earned her college degree in Art Education, and, as a little girl, I reaped the benefits of her training. In the years before I started kindergarten, we spent several mornings a week with the *Creations for Kids* book in front of us, inspiring our projects. On top of wax paper that Mom meticulously taped to the surface of the kitchen table, we worked side by side to make tie-dyed wrapping paper for birthday gifts, crayon batiks to decorate the walls, papier mâché masks for Halloween, and bread-dough ornaments at Christmas. When I created elaborate wads of dough too heavy

to hang and wrapping paper that was nearly black from the number of paints into which I dipped it, Mom helped me to make subtle changes yet keep my ideas intact. In the years that followed, she continued to encourage my dreams but ensure my practicality. I count among my best decisions the ones I made with her help. Her advice is so familiar to me that it is now a gentle inner voice, still steering me to create and consider. I can hear her wise and loving words, even when she's not working beside me.

A MOTHER'S LOVE . . .

guides

FLYING HIGH

Ramona Pope Richards

What do you think of when you hear the word 'mother'?" I was asked recently. I think of courage and independence and understanding. These were the gifts she gave to me, and they are not easily represented by objects.

"Try it for yourself," she said. "You'll never know if you don't try. Just remember, I'll always be here if you fail." This advice helped me through the roughest times of my life. It gave me the independence and courage I needed as a college freshman, as a new bride, as a new mother. As with most motherly advice, I had to grow up to understand and

appreciate it. Only as an adult did I realize how hard it was for Mother to stand back and let me try things for myself. She was always there to comfort the pain of failure, but more importantly, she was brave enough to let the pain occur.

She taught me to fly while she held the net. The only way I can repay her is to fly high above the net and pass on to my own children the gifts of courage, understanding, and independence she gave me. Flowers just aren't enough.

The future destiny of the child is always the work of the mother.

—Napoleon

Into the woman's keeping is committed the destiny of the generations to come after us.

—Theodore Roosevelt

[A mother's] most important function is that of teacher. Not a teacher in the classroom sense, but a teacher of the fundamental values of life.

—GEORGE J. HECHT

It's an impossible job
No one can ever do it perfectly
Be willing to accept that there
is no success or failure here
Let us give up the burden of
unreal expectations
Let us cherish what is and
nourish each other's dreams

LET US REMEMBER THE BEST
AND FORGIVE THE REST
ALLOW ALL THE LOVE THAT MAY HAVE
SLIPPED INTO TIGHT PLACES FREE NOW
TO ILLUMINATE THE HARMONY
THAT ALWAYS EXISTED
AT THE VERY CENTER
OF OUR HEARTS
—ARLENE GAY LEVINE

A MOTHER'S
LOVE . . .

we

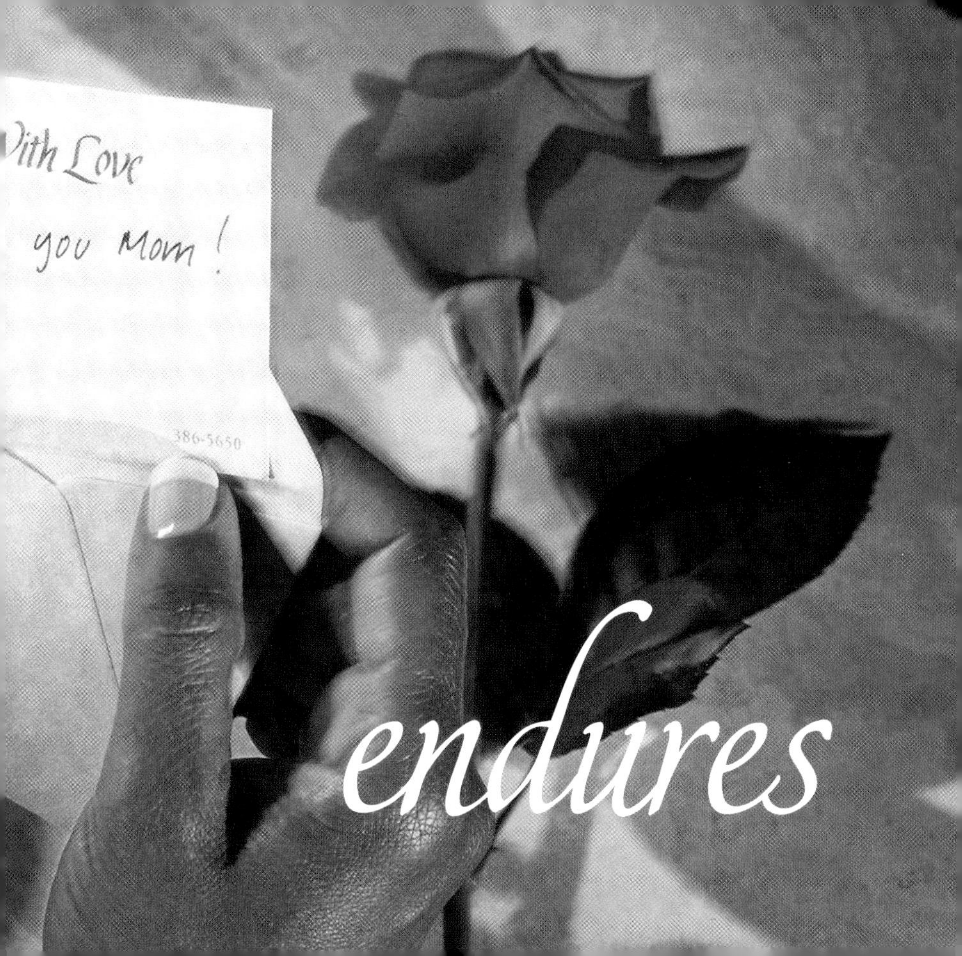

endures

Though distance may come
between a mother and her child,
the bond that holds them close
will never weaken—
the love they share
will never be more
than a memory apart.

—DEAN WALLEY

As an only child, I spent lots of time with my mother. She was there in the morning when I awoke, and she regularly tucked me in at night. In between we took walks, read books, played with dolls, and talked about all kinds of things. She taught me to ride a bike, swim, sew, and make pies. And in addition to all this, she demonstrated in large and small ways how to be caring and compassionate to others, how to be assertive without being obnoxious. She gave me the confidence to be myself and the forgiveness I needed to grow from my mistakes. In short, she was, and still is, my good friend.

—Pamela Kennedy

RECONNECTING

Beth Livermore

Some women reconnect over long walks and fireside chats. For Mom and me, it was an eight-day trip to Tanzania. . . . Besides executing a successful trip and sharing a grand adventure, we reclaimed common ground that had eroded with separation. And for the first time in years I was reminded of my mom's role in shaping who I've become.

She was, after all, the one who ignited my wanderlust with her own desire to see the Grand Canyon, the Alhambra, and Vermont in autumn. She taught me the rewards of pushing the envelope by going first into a freezing mountain river for the swim of a lifetime. And how often do I repeat her simple, but potent, maxims when I need a kick in the pants? "Don't get lazy. It's the extra effort that makes life worthwhile," says a woman who drove three kids across America in a tent camper to see the country—and thereby changed our lives. "Why not take a chance? You could fall down the stairs and break your neck." I used that one to get on a plane to Antarctica. Still none of this was apparent until we traveled

together as two fully grown women. Now a mother myself, who must constantly choose between safety and opportunity, necessity and whim, I cherish these gifts more than ever.

ALWAYS THERE

Cokie Roberts

Mamma could always be counted on to come through. Intellectually, I know that she was actually away a lot of the time when we were growing up. She was off campaigning for Daddy, or accompanying him on some official trip. She always worked, for him, for the party, for the community. Even so, as I resurrect those childhood pictures in my memory, they all include Mamma. To me, she was the most beautiful woman on earth, and she seemed a constant presence. . . .

OUR HEARTBEATS, NOTES
EACH SEPARATE, BUT PART OF THE
SAME MELODY.
THE LYRICS OF OUR LIVES
INTERTWINED,
COMPOSED OF LOVE,
WILL BE SUNG FOR GENERATIONS.
—CHERYL MORIKAWA